WONDER

by
R.J. Palacio

Teacher Guide

Written by
Mina Watts

Note

The 2012 Alfred A. Knopf hardcover edition of the novel, © 2012 by R.J. Palacio, was used to prepare this guide. The page references may differ in other editions. Novel ISBN: 978-0-375-86902-0

Please note: Parts of this novel deal with sensitive, mature issues. Please assess the appropriateness of this novel for the age level and maturity of your students prior to reading and discussing it with them.

ISBN 978-1-56137-976-7

To order, contact your local school supply store, or—

Novel Units, Inc.
P.O. Box 97
Bulverde, TX 78163-0097

Web site: novelunits.com

Table of Contents

Skills and Strategies

Critical Thinking

Predictions, analysis, inferences, research, supporting judgments, compare/contrast, pros/cons

Comprehension

Cause/effect, summarizing, identifying attributes

Literary Elements

Epigraphs, allusions, theme, character analysis, figurative language, author's purpose, point of view, symbolism, conflict/resolution

Vocabulary

Definitions, application, word maps, dictionary entries

Listening/Speaking

Discussion, presentation, skit

Writing

Journal entry, alternate ending, essay, poem, newspaper review

Across the Curriculum

Music—"Wonder" by Natalie Merchant, zydeco music, baroque violin vs. hardanger fiddle; Art—collage, watercolor, chalk drawing, pencil sketch, brochure, comic strip; Health—cleft lip/cleft palate, tics, bullying; Entertainment/Popular Culture—*Doogie Howser, M.D.*, *Star Wars*, *Auggie Doggie and Doggie Daddy* cartoon; Literature—*Diary of a Wimpy Kid* by Jeff Kinney, novels about children with differences; Science—acids and bases, Punnett squares

Genre: realistic fiction

Setting: North River Heights (a fictional neighborhood in Manhattan, New York)

Point of View: multiple first person

Themes: identity, individuality, belonging, acceptance, unconditional love, family, bullying, friendship, coming of age, kindness, human relationships

Conflict: person vs. self, person vs. society, person vs. person

Style: narrative from multiple perspectives (with occasional flashbacks)

Tone: poignant, candid, conversational, often humorous

Date of First Publication: 2012

Summary

August (Auggie) Pullman is nervous about starting fifth grade at Beecher Prep—but not for the reasons most kids are nervous. Auggie was born with a rare facial deformity that instantly draws people's attention. For this reason, Auggie was homeschooled his entire life, but now Auggie's parents feel that he should attend regular school so he can socialize with other children his age. So, Auggie braves Beecher Prep, a local private school, and soon realizes that children his age can be unkind—even downright cruel. But he also finds allies in people like Summer, a genuinely kind girl who sees past Auggie's deformity to his true character, and Jack Will, a boy who learns much about himself because of Auggie. With the support of his loving parents and older sister Via, Auggie perseveres at Beecher Prep until, one day, things begin changing in his favor. The multiple perspectives of Via, Summer, Jack, and others provide insight not only into Auggie's birth, upbringing, and everyday challenges, but also into the lives of everyone he encounters. Because of his struggles, Auggie discovers a strength he never knew he possessed. Armed with new knowledge and experience, he begins the next chapter of his life.

About the Author

R.J. Palacio grew up in a working-class neighborhood in Queens, New York. The writer, whose real name is Raquel Jaramillo, uses her mother's last name as her pen name. Palacio's Colombian-born mother surrounded her daughter with books and encouraged her authorial efforts, saying, "...remember, you're a writer." Palacio worked as an art director and book jacket designer for over 20 years, creating covers for a variety of genres and authors. She waited for the perfect time to write her own book but soon realized that "it's never the perfect time to start writing a book." After that realization, Palacio began writing *Wonder*, her first novel. Of the book's cover, Palacio says: "...I didn't design [it], but I sure do love it." While she has received much praise for *Wonder*, Palacio feels the most important praise she received was from her 15-year-old son, who loved the novel and claimed that it should be required reading for anyone entering middle school. Palacio currently lives in New York City with her husband, two sons, and two dogs.

Background Information

1. **Inspiration for the novel:** Palacio traces her inspiration for *Wonder* back to an incident that occurred outside an ice cream shop when her sons were 11 and three years old. Palacio's older son went into the shop to purchase milkshakes, while Palacio and her younger son waited outside. Suddenly, Palacio's younger son appeared frightened and began to cry. A little girl with a severe facial deformity, along with her mother and another girl, was sitting next to Palacio. Palacio, unsure of how to react, quickly gathered her sons and left. Later, Palacio considered what the little girl's life must be like. Realizing she had reacted badly and thus missed one of life's "teachable moments," Palacio decided that she and her children, as well as many other people, might need to learn some more positive ways to react in such situations. That same night, Palacio heard the song "Wonder" by Natalie Merchant on the radio, and, as Palacio says, "something about the words to the song just got to me." She began writing *Wonder* that night, a novel that is not about bullying or fitting in, but rather about choosing kindness above all else.

2. **Auggie's deformity:** Auggie's medical condition is never given a specific name, though many details are given about his physical appearance. Palacio intended it that way, saying, "I didn't want to make it specifically any syndrome—I think it's almost unimportant." Palacio did not seek advice from medical professionals while writing the novel, either. Instead, she conducted her own research online and by watching documentaries. Palacio emphasizes that explaining Auggie's condition is not the focus of the novel. Auggie is intended as a metaphor for "anyone who's different, anyone who's not part of the crowd and has any sort of special need." In *Wonder*'s Acknowledgments, Palacio thanks "the little girl in front of the ice cream shop and all the other 'Auggies'" (p. 315) for inspiring her to write the novel.

Characters

August (Auggie) Pullman: fifth-grade boy; born with facial deformities that necessitate frequent surgeries; warm-hearted, intelligent, funny child who feels like an outcast because of his physical appearance; begins attending private school in fifth grade

Olivia (Via) Pullman: Auggie's sister; high-school freshman; defends Auggie fiercely; has always accepted that Auggie requires more of her parents' attention, but nonetheless feels emotionally neglected by them

Isabel Pullman: Auggie's mother; protective of Auggie; loving and compassionate; favors allowing Auggie to socialize but constantly worries about how others will treat him

Nate Pullman: Auggie's father; protective of Auggie; humorous; favors sheltering Auggie over allowing him to experience the world on his own

Summer Dawson: brown-haired, green-eyed classmate of Auggie's; befriends Auggie on his first day at school; chooses kindness over popularity

Jack Will: friendly, outgoing classmate of Auggie's; lives with his family in a lower-income area of North River Heights; asked by Mr. Tushman to befriend Auggie; betrays Auggie but wins his friendship back

Amanda Will: Jack's mother; kind person who takes pride in her sons' accomplishments

Julian Albans: popular, mean-spirited classmate of Auggie's; constantly takes subtle jabs at Auggie's appearance; turns other classmates against Auggie but is ultimately rejected by his own friends

Melissa Albans: Julian's mother; narrow-minded, petty woman who questions whether Auggie belongs at Beecher Prep

Charlotte Cody: friendly classmate of Auggie's; very intelligent

Henry Joplin: large boy who is friends with Julian and initially treats Auggie badly; becomes one of Auggie's protectors by the end of the novel

Miles Noury: boy who is friends with Julian and initially treats Auggie badly; eventually rallies to Auggie's defense

Amos Conti: boy who initially ignores Auggie; eventually defends Auggie and replaces Julian in the social scene

Reid, Ximena, Maya, Tristan, Max G., Max W.: other fifth graders at Beecher Prep

Justin: boy whom Via begins dating; shocked by Auggie's appearance but quickly adjusts to and accepts Auggie; has neglectful parents

Miranda Navas: Via's friend since childhood; spent a summer apart from Via and changed her appearance drastically; shares a special bond with Auggie

Mr. Tushman: director of the middle school at Beecher Prep; kind and understanding; goes to lengths to help Auggie feel at home in his new school

Mrs. Garcia: Mr. Tushman's assistant; genuinely kind to Auggie

Ms. Petosa: Auggie's homeroom teacher

Mr. Browne: Auggie's English teacher; offers students "precepts," or mottos by which to live their lives

Mr. Roche: Auggie's history teacher

Christopher, Zachary, and Alex: Auggie's friends since childhood; The four boys grew apart after Christopher moved away and they began attending different schools.

Lisa: Christopher's mother

Initiating Activities

Use one or more of the following to introduce the novel.

1. Literary Devices: Have students read the epigraphs on the novel's divider pages for Parts One–Eight. Students should research four of these allusions (references to other works) and discuss how they think their four selected allusions will relate to the novel's themes.

2. Predictions: Have students study the illustrations included on the novel's divider pages for Parts One–Eight. Then, students should predict how the illustrations will relate to the characters in the novel.

3. Journal Entry: Ask students to think about a time when they tried something new and potentially frightening (e.g., rode a particular roller coaster, learned to ride a bike, visited a different city/state/country). Have students write a journal entry describing their feelings before and after the event, as well as whether they were glad they did it.

4. Author's Purpose: Use the Internet to find the lyrics to Natalie Merchant's song "Wonder." In two to three paragraphs, students should discuss why this song was so inspiring to the novel's author.

5. Predictions: Have students complete the I Predict... activity on page 24 of this guide.

6. Opinion Essay: Have students compose a short essay agreeing or disagreeing with one of the following statements.

   a) Even kind people commit cruel acts that they later regret.

   b) Fitting in is easy; standing out from the crowd is difficult.

   c) Parents should always pay the same amount of attention to each of their children.

Vocabulary Activities

1. Vocabulary Collage: Have students search in magazines, newspapers, and online for pictures and words related to themes in *Wonder*, such as unconditional love, friendship, belonging, and kindness. Students should create collages to represent their ideas.

2. Word Map: Have students complete word maps like the one on page 25 of this guide for the following words: obnoxious, exception, emphatically, mutual, interjects.

3. Predictive Sequencing: Randomly write the following vocabulary words on the board: petrified, forewarned, aversion, bizarre, transition, resolute, defensively, mayhem. Discuss the meaning of each word, and have students write the words in the order they think they might appear in the novel. Discuss the reasons for students' sequencing choices.

4. Word Skits: Divide students into groups, and assign five vocabulary words to each group. Students should write skits that incorporate the meanings of the vocabulary words into their stories as well as use the words in dialogue.

5. Vocabulary Dictionary: Students should choose ten vocabulary words from the lists in this guide, and create a dictionary entry for each. Entries should include the word, any alternate spellings, the word's part of speech, the language from which the word originated (if applicable), and the correct pronunciation(s) for the word. Students should then share their "mini-dictionary" with the class.

6. Picture This: Assign each student a vocabulary word from the lists in this guide. In small groups, have students take turns drawing pictures that represent their assigned words. (Students may not give spoken clues.) The first group to guess all of their team members' words is the winner.

Ordinary–Locks

Auggie Pullman introduces himself as "not an ordinary ten-year-old kid" (p. 3). He relates how his facial deformity often startles adults and frightens children. Auggie, however, has grown accustomed to such reactions, as have his family members. The severity of Auggie's birth defects was unanticipated, his appearance shocking even the doctor. As a child, Auggie underwent frequent operations, making homeschooling necessary. Now, as he enters fifth grade, Auggie faces a new set of challenges as he enrolls in a "normal" school for the first time. At the exclusive Beecher Prep, Auggie warms to Mr. Tushman, the school's friendly principal, but is uncertain about interacting with his peers. On his first day of school, Auggie nervously sits in Ms. Petosa's homeroom class, awaiting his fate.

Vocabulary
extraordinary
petrified
surgeries
hysterical
hindsight
electives
percussion
baritone
incubator
sarcastically
obnoxious
forewarned

Discussion Questions

1. How is Auggie ordinary, yet not ordinary? (*Auggie is ordinary in that he acts like a typical ten-year-old—he likes ice cream, rides a bike, enjoys sports, and plays video games. However, Auggie also has an unusual appearance and realizes that "ordinary kids don't make other ordinary kids run away screaming" or "get stared at wherever they go" [p. 3].*)

2. How do Auggie's family members react when people are startled by Auggie's appearance? What do you think their reactions demonstrate about them? (*Like Auggie, his parents "know how to pretend [they] don't see the faces people make" [p. 3]. In short, they have learned to ignore or overlook people's negative reactions to Auggie's appearance. In contrast, Auggie's sister Via cannot ignore people's responses to Auggie. She is irritated by people's rudeness and inability to suppress their reactions. She fiercely defends Auggie, especially against cruel children. Answers will vary, but students should note that Auggie's family loves him unconditionally. His parents and Via have dealt with these types of reactions for ten years, and each chooses to respond differently. Via's responses may indicate a particularly strong bond with Auggie, as Via is closest in age to Auggie and likely knows how cruel young people can be to someone who is different.*)

3. How does Auggie's mom describe Auggie's birth? Why do you think she describes it in this way? (*Auggie's mom tells the story humorously, giving the most focus to the "farting nurse" and "fainting doctor" in the delivery room. She also emphasizes that when she saw Auggie's face for the first time, "all she could see was how pretty [his] eyes were" [p. 7]. Answers will vary, but students should infer that Auggie's mom wishes to convey that she has always loved Auggie, despite his deformities and changing appearance since birth. Some students may speculate that Auggie's mom exaggerated [or made up] certain funny elements to downplay the seriousness of Auggie's condition and the shock of the hospital staff.*)

4. Why do Auggie's parents disagree about whether Auggie is ready to attend school? Discuss how each parent's view reflects concern for Auggie's well-being. (*Auggie's mom feels that her son needs more support and knowledge than she can provide. She is also concerned that she and her husband are sheltering Auggie from the real world by avoiding uncomfortable situations and unfamiliar people. Auggie's dad feels that sending Auggie to school is like "sending…a lamb to the slaughter" [p. 10]. He is afraid that Auggie's spirit will be destroyed by people's judgment, misconceptions, and fear of the unfamiliar. Answers will vary. Auggie's mom shows concern for his social and mental development, whereas Auggie's dad seems more worried about his son's emotional needs.*)

5. How does Auggie's initial meeting with Mr. Tushman differ from his initial meeting with Mrs. Garcia? Why do you think Auggie notices this slight difference? *(When Auggie meets Mr. Tushman, he notices that the principal looks directly at him, smiles, and extends his hand for Auggie to shake. Mr. Tushman also makes a point of kneeling before Auggie to address him face-to-face. When Auggie meets Mrs. Garcia, he notices that she does something that Auggie is accustomed to: she drops her eyes and smiles "a really shiny smile" [p. 17]. She is kind to Auggie, complimenting his firm handshake and offering to assist him with anything he needs. Answers will vary. Auggie has grown up looking different than everyone around him, and therefore he is highly sensitive to others' reactions to his appearance. He can "read" people extremely well and senses when someone feels uncomfortable in his presence. Students should note that Auggie still likes Mrs. Garcia, just not her "shiny smile.")*

6. How does Auggie use his hair as a defense mechanism (something that helps a person cope with uncomfortable or frightening situations)? *(Auggie explains that he grew his hair out so that his bangs would cover his eyes, helping him "block out the things [he doesn't] want to see" [p. 21]. Though Auggie is aware of others' negative reactions to his appearance, he frequently chooses to ignore such reactions rather than giving people the satisfaction of knowing they hurt his feelings.)*

7. How do Jack Will, Julian, and Charlotte act toward Auggie? How do Julian's words and actions differ from Jack Will's and Charlotte's? *(Jack Will speaks matter-of-factly and acts slightly stiff. Charlotte speaks animatedly and is extremely energetic. Julian speaks indifferently and seems mean-spirited. Unlike Jack Will and Charlotte, Julian purposely tries to make Auggie feel foolish and inexperienced. He laughs at Auggie's uncertainty, stares openly at Auggie's face, and asks him, "What's the deal with your face? I mean, were you in a fire or something" [p. 29]? At the end of the tour, Julian intentionally blocks Auggie's path and apologizes, though Auggie notes from Julian's expression that Julian "wasn't really sorry at all" [p. 30].)*

8. Why do you think Auggie's mom and dad change their opinions about whether Auggie should attend school? *(Answers will vary. Though Auggie's mom initially thought school was an enlightening experience that Auggie needed, she seems rattled by Julian's candid questions about Auggie's appearance. Her protective instincts have most likely caused her to change her opinion. Auggie's father initially did not believe Auggie was ready for school, but he seems heartened by how Auggie handled an uncomfortable situation. He is not as worried as a result of Auggie's show of strength.)*

9. Why is the first day of school a particularly stressful experience for Auggie? *(In addition to the worries of any student [e.g., anxiety about finding one's classes, making friends, having the correct supplies, meeting new teachers], Auggie has never attended a real school before. And, as always, Auggie is apprehensive about how people will react to his appearance.)*

10. How is Auggie treated on his first day of school? *(Though some people are kind to Auggie [e.g., Ms. Petosa, Charlotte, and Jack Will], others are not. For example, a boy named Henry Joplin insists on sharing a desk with another student so he will not have to sit next to Auggie. When asked by Ms. Petosa to move to the empty desk next to Auggie, he does so sluggishly and "[plops] his backpack up really high on the right side of the desk so it was kind of like a wall" [p. 39]. As expected, Auggie feels "everyone's eyes burning into [his] back" [p. 39] in homeroom.)*

11. **Prediction:** How will Auggie adapt to Beecher Prep?

Supplementary Activities

1. Character Analysis: Begin the Character Web on page 26 of this guide for Auggie. Continue to fill in information as you read.

2. Health/Research: Using your school library or online resources, find information about the conditions known as cleft lip and cleft palate. Then, research organizations that fund and perform operations to correct these conditions (e.g., Operation Smile). Write a one- to two-page report with your findings.

3. Popular Culture: Research the TV character Doogie Howser. As a class, discuss why Auggie's parents might have nicknamed the delivery room doctor "Doogie."

Around the Room–Names

Auggie braves his first day of school, though he feels he is on display. To his surprise, Auggie realizes he is going to enjoy school. The high point of his first day is eating lunch with Summer, a smart, sunny girl who genuinely seems to want to be Auggie's friend. Auggie also feels he has found a true friend in Jack Will. Auggie's birthday party at a local bowling alley is a success, even though a significant portion of the invited guests do not attend. On Halloween, Auggie changes his costume at the last minute, arriving at school as the "Bleeding Scream" rather than Boba Fett, his planned costume. Effectively disguised, Auggie hears Jack Will making nasty comments about him. Crushed, Auggie fakes a stomach ache and is sent home early by the school nurse.

Vocabulary
pursue
motivate
plaque
alignment
prehistoric
exception
straggle
coincidence
mortality
aversion

Discussion Questions

1. How does Julian cunningly insult Auggie while faking interest in *Star Wars*? Why do you think the chapter ends with the words, "Yeah, he knew what he was saying" (p. 44)? *(After establishing that Ms. Petosa is not familiar with* Star Wars, *Julian asks Auggie if he likes the character Darth Sidious—who just happens to be a character with a deformed, melted face. In this way, Julian insults Auggie without their teacher detecting it. Answers will vary. After peering at Julian, Auggie realizes that Julian "knew what he was saying" [p. 44], or, in other words, was being intentionally hurtful. Auggie's heightened awareness of others' intentions shows that he is accustomed to people being spiteful and insensitive toward him.)*

2. Judging from Mr. Tushman's, Ms. Petosa's, and Mr. Browne's words and actions, how might the staff at Beecher Prep best be described? Do you think having these types of adult role models will help Auggie adjust to his new school? Why or why not? *(Answers will vary. The staff at Beecher Prep is incredibly kind, very focused, and extremely energetic. Each teacher [or principal] seems excited about his or her new students and is very welcoming and open-minded. Though having these types of adults around will likely help Auggie, students should note that some of Auggie's peers lack the kindness and tact the adults at Beecher Prep demonstrate. The adults make up only half of the equation.)*

3. Why does lunchtime make Auggie feel more conspicuous than he already did? What improves his lunch drastically? *(Auggie eats differently than most children, since a hole remains in the roof of his mouth. He chews using only the front of his mouth, and though he has had numerous surgeries on his face, his meals can still get messy. Auggie's first-day lunch is vastly improved when a friendly girl named Summer sits down at Auggie's table and begins talking to him.)*

4. How do you think Auggie's mom feels when she picks up Auggie after his first day of school? *(Answers will vary, but Auggie's mom is probably extremely nervous since Auggie attending a "normal" school was her idea. She constantly worries about how others will treat Auggie, whom she*

has always protected. Now that Auggie's experiences are out of her hands, apprehension has set in. On the other hand, Auggie's mom may also be excited to see her son beginning a new chapter in his life.)

5. Why do you think Auggie cries as his mother reads to him? *(Answers will vary, but students should recognize that Auggie's first day of school put a great deal of pressure on him. Auggie's mom is also reading a particularly dismal passage from* The Hobbit, *which describes a "gloomy party" and a "path [that] seemed to straggle on just as before [with] no change" [p. 59]. Perhaps the gloomy passage made Auggie feel hopeless, since he knows that he cannot change his appearance and will never "fit in" in the classical sense.)*

6. Why is September a particularly difficult month for Auggie? *(September serves as Auggie's adjustment period for school. He must adapt to getting up early, doing homework, taking quizzes, and having less free time. In addition, Auggie must endure people staring at him and whispering about him constantly as they grow accustomed to his appearance.)*

7. Do you think Auggie is genuinely amused by Jack's comment that Auggie "should sue [his] doctor" (p. 64)? Why or why not? *(Answers will vary. While some students might think that Auggie laughing along with Jack is only a defense mechanism, most students will probably realize that Auggie possesses a unique self-awareness. As Auggie expresses, he wants to tell other kids, "…it's okay, [I] know I'm weird-looking, take a look, I don't bite" [p. 62]. Auggie can also distinguish between a mean-spirited comment and a good-natured one. He is comfortable enough with Jack that he can laugh at himself, and Jack obviously feels close enough to Auggie to joke around with him freely.)*

8. Why does Auggie invite his entire homeroom class to his birthday party? What do you think his classmates' responses reflect about them? *(Auggie invites every student in his homeroom class because he doesn't "want anyone to get their feelings hurt if they find out other people are invited and they aren't" [p. 66]. Auggie knows what feeling left out is like, and he is reluctant to impose that feeling on anyone else. Answers will vary. The people Auggie considers his closest friends [Summer and Jack Will] most likely responded "yes" first, and several other kids RSVP or say they will try to attend. Students should note that everyone Auggie invited responded, whether their answer was "yes" or "no," except for Julian.)*

9. What does Auggie notice about his classmates first in dance class and then during his science elective? Why doesn't this realization rattle Auggie? *(Auggie notices that "even though people were getting used to [him], no one would actually touch [him]" [p. 71]. He observes Ximena Chin's panic when she is assigned to be Auggie's dance partner and Tristan's meltdown when Auggie accidentally touches his hand in the science lab. Answers will vary, but most students will likely conclude that Auggie, unfortunately, is accustomed to being singled out and embarrassed because of his physical differences.)*

10. Why is Halloween Auggie's favorite holiday? *(Auggie loves Halloween because it enables him to wear a costume and mask and trick-or-treat like every other kid. It is immensely freeing for Auggie to feel normal for just one day. Auggie expresses his wish that every day was Halloween so people "could walk around and get to know each other before we got to see what we looked like" [p. 73]. For Auggie, Halloween is the one time every year when he faces no judgment.)*

11. How does Auggie's last-minute costume change affect his enjoyment of Halloween? *(Since Auggie had announced that he would be Boba Fett for Halloween, no one knows who he is when he arrives in a Bleeding Scream costume. Still in disguise, Auggie overhears three boys saying horribly mean things about him and, to his shock, Auggie realizes that one of the boys is Jack Will. Stunned and upset, Auggie finds his way to the nurse's office and is sent home, declining even to go trick-or-treating later.)*

12. **Prediction:** How will Auggie treat Jack Will when he returns to school?

Supplementary Activities

1. Entertainment: Research the following *Star Wars* references, and then tell how each is important in the novel's context: Padawan, Jedi, Jango Fett, Darth Sidious, Boba Fett, clone trooper, Obi-Wan Kenobi, Darth Vader.

2. Science: Look up the scientific terms "acid" and "base." Then, use a T-chart to classify the following everyday substances as either acids or bases: lemon juice, baking soda, mustard, vinegar, coffee, orange juice, toothpaste, aspirin, yogurt.

3. Literature: Read *Diary of a Wimpy Kid* by Jeff Kinney. In one to two paragraphs, explain the origin of the "Cheese Touch." Discuss whether you think Auggie's comparison is a good one.

A Tour of the Galaxy–The Egyptian Tomb

Via describes living in Auggie's shadow, including the sacrifices she has made and the guilt she often feels. Now in high school, Via is drifting away from her old friends, Miranda and Ella. Though Via knows her problems could never eclipse Auggie's, she still yearns for more of her parents' attention. Via also discusses the likelihood that she or Auggie will have a child with Auggie's condition. Via decides to cut ties altogether with Miranda and Ella, which affects her more than she realizes. The novel then shifts to Summer's point of view as she highlights Auggie's many redeeming qualities. When Summer is invited to a popular girl's party, she is excited—that is, until people at the party attempt to convince her to ditch Auggie. Despite setbacks, Summer and Auggie remain close friends.

Vocabulary
celestial
disproportionately
catastrophe
bizarre
dynamics
obsession
decisively
exotic
transition
emphatically
literally
platoon
caption

Discussion Questions

1. Why does Via claim that "this year there seems to be a shift in the cosmos" and "planets are falling out of alignment" (p. 83)? *(Answers will vary. The shift Via is referring to might relate to the fact that both she and Auggie are starting different schools, with Auggie attending a real school for the first time. Via might also be implying that she plans to demand more of her parents' attention now that Auggie's health is relatively stable.)*

2. Describe the "two Augusts" that Via mentions. What do Via's ponderings about the "two Augusts" demonstrate about her? *(The "two Augusts" are two different views of her brother that Via has experienced. One is the Auggie she has always known—a fun-loving, affectionate, tough little brother. The other is the Auggie other people see—a child with a terrible deformity. Answers will vary. Though Via hates herself for viewing Auggie—even for a second—as strangers do, her thoughts demonstrate that she is an intelligent, compassionate girl who seeks to understand all viewpoints.)*

3. What did Via love the most about middle school and, now, high school? *(Via loved that her middle school "was separate and different from home" [p. 91]. Since everyone in her elementary school knew Auggie and her parents, Via enjoyed the relative anonymity middle school afforded her. Now, in high school, Via relishes the fact that no one knows her or Auggie. In effect, she has a clean slate. She is not ashamed of Auggie; rather, she wishes to have an identity independent of any of her family members.)*

4. Why do you think Via avoids telling her mother about the "new Miranda"? *(Answers will vary, but it seems that Via is being as selfless as always. She assumes Auggie has bigger problems, so she keeps hers to herself. She also knows how much her parents worry on a regular basis, and she probably does not want to add to their burden. Perhaps she also suspects she will be scolded for taking the subway home alone.)*

5. Why do you think Mr. Pullman pushes for Via to be allowed to take the subway alone? *(Answers will vary, but Via's dad seems to realize that Via is very mature for her age—both emotionally and mentally. He tells his wife, "Isabel, she can take the subway!...She's reading* War and Peace, *for crying out loud" [p. 101]. His support might also stem from his inside knowledge about Via's current clash with Miranda and Ella.)*

6. What can the reader conclude about Via based on her knowledge of the Pullmans' genetics? *(Answers will vary. Via has obviously listened when doctors talked to her parents about their "genetic lottery," and perhaps she has conducted research on her own. She remembers the labels doctors have given Auggie's many afflictions and enjoys "how doctors talk" and "the sound of science" [p. 106]. Via has contemplated both her and Auggie's futures, calculating the chances of their family's mutated gene affecting the next generation. It seems that Via has already concluded that she will not have children, grouping her would-be offspring with the "countless babies who'll never be born" [p. 106].)*

7. How does this particular Halloween bring Via and Auggie closer together? *(Despite having her own problems, Via is concerned that Auggie feels too sick to trick-or-treat—his favorite thing in the world. The two are drawn closer together when Auggie confesses what he overheard Jack and Julian saying about him. Via knows her brother well enough to allow him a few minutes to expel his anger, then attempt to cheer him up by taking him to the Halloween parade. Since school started, the siblings had grown apart somewhat, but having an honest conversation on Halloween cements their relationship once again.)*

8. Why is Summer surprised by the attention she gets for being friends with Auggie? *(Summer seems to have a different, less shallow perspective than most of her peers. She is friends with Auggie because she enjoys his company. However, Summer's classmates cannot grasp the idea that a pretty, smart girl like Summer would voluntarily spend time with an outcast. Charlotte even questions whether Mr. Tushman asked Summer to befriend Auggie.)*

9. Why do you think Summer is excited to attend Savanna's party, and why might Savanna have invited her? *(Though Summer is not terribly concerned with popularity, even she admits she feels special to have been invited to such an exclusive party. Plus, Summer seems like the type of person who hates to snub others and is open to friendships with anyone. Answers will vary, but from Henry's and Savanna's comments, it seems Summer was invited to the party either to [1] be embarrassed about her friendship with Auggie or [2] be talked out of associating with him.)*

10. How does Auggie's explanation of his deformity to Summer demonstrate his strong spirit? *(Auggie's nonchalant, witty answer to Summer's unspoken question about his face hints that he has answered the question before and is no longer hurt when people ask it. He is knowledgeable about his condition, rattling off many medical terms at one point, but he is good-natured enough to end his explanation on a mischievous note to spare Summer any discomfort. Auggie's strong spirit shines when he speaks in this way, demonstrating that he accepts his reality.)*

11. **Prediction:** How might Jack get Auggie to forgive him?

Supplementary Activities

1. Art: Using Via's metaphor in which Auggie is the Sun (see page 82 of the novel), create a visual representation of the Pullman "galaxy," labeling each part with a person's name and what they represent (e.g., Via—a planet).

2. Comprehension: Review the family history Via relates on page 103 of the novel. Beginning with Auggie and Via Pullman, create a family tree for the Pullmans.

3. Science: Use library resources or the Internet to find information about Punnett squares. Then, complete a Punnett square for the child of two people with alleles Bb and bb, where Bb = brown eyes and bb = blue eyes. Answer the following questions:

   a. What is the likelihood that the child will have brown eyes?

   b. What is the likelihood that the child will have blue eyes?

   c. What is the likelihood that the child will be a carrier for allele b (i.e., will carry the recessive trait for blue eyes)?

The Call–The Boyfriend

Jack confesses his initial reluctance to befriend Auggie at Mr. Tushman's request and tells how he changed his mind when he realized the difficulties Auggie would be facing. Jack describes his family's tight finances and modest lifestyle, which often separates Jack from his wealthier classmates. He realizes Auggie heard him gossiping with Julian on Halloween, and after Julian makes yet another rude comment about Auggie, Jack's anger boils over. He punches Julian and refuses to say why he did it. Jack and Auggie mend their friendship, while Julian turns most of the boys at Beecher Prep against Jack. One day, while Auggie and Jack are working on their science project at the Pullmans' house, Via enters and introduces them to her new boyfriend, Justin.

Vocabulary
alabaster
kinetic
inkling
valid
retrospect
stringent
protocol
resolute
mutual
hypocrite
addiction
organic

Discussion Questions

1. How did Jack react to Auggie the first time he saw him? What did his babysitter mean when she said, "...sometimes you don't have to mean to hurt someone to hurt someone" (p. 137)? (*Jack cried out in surprise and left immediately with his babysitter, asking her in a whisper what was wrong with the boy he saw. Answers will vary, but Veronica was most likely trying to stress that the boy, his mother, and his sister probably each felt upset after seeing Jack's reaction, even though it was unintentional. Just because Jack "didn't mean it" [p. 137] did not mean the boy's feelings weren't hurt.*)

2. Why does Jack agree to help Mr. Tushman? What can the reader infer about Jack based on this decision? (*Jack realizes that "if a little kid like Jamie, who's usually a nice enough kid, can be that mean, then a kid like August doesn't stand a chance in middle school" [p. 141]. In other words, Jack decides that Auggie can use all the allies he can get. Answers will vary. Though Jack initially wants to turn Mr. Tushman down, he considers the situation from Auggie's viewpoint, proving that Jack is sympathetic and compassionate. Perhaps Jack, who feels set apart by his family's financial hardship, can identify with Auggie's loneliness.*)

3. Why is Jack first thrilled about, but later ashamed of, his refurbished sled? *(Initially, Jack is excited about the sled because he found it abandoned in the park, fixed it up himself using household materials and leftover spray paint, and named it* Lightning. *The sled is faster and sturdier than any sled Jack has ever owned. However, back at school, Jack discovers that* Lightning *was originally Miles's old sled—which Miles calls a "piece of junk" [p. 150]. Jack is humiliated to realize that the nicest sled he has ever owned was someone else's garbage.)*

4. Why does Jack punch Julian? Why do you think he refuses to tell Mr. Tushman the real reasons for his actions? *(Jack punches Julian in defense of Auggie after Julian once again insults Auggie by calling him "that freak." Julian also attempts to "save" Jack from partnering with Auggie on Ms. Rubin's science project, even after Jack tells him to drop the issue. It also seems that Jack is angry with himself for bad-mouthing Auggie to impress Julian. Jack's anger at himself and at Julian's poor behavior seems to erupt all at once. Answers will vary. As Jack says, "some things you just can't explain" [p. 155]. Jack also knows that if he repeats what Julian said about Auggie after science class, Julian will repeat what Jack said about Auggie on Halloween. Jack seems to feel conflicted, but not necessarily regretful that he punched Julian.)*

5. Why does Mrs. Albans email Mr. Tushman? Why do you think Mr. Tushman responds as he does? *(Mrs. Albans emails Mr. Tushman supposedly to express her approval of the measures taken against Jack. However, Mrs. Albans's real agenda becomes clearer as she claims that the "pressure" placed on Jack to be friends with Auggie is to blame for Jack's violent actions. She also expresses being "disturbed" that Auggie was allowed to interview off-site and attend Beecher Prep at all. Answers will vary. Mr. Tushman's response to Mrs. Albans's email is firm, yet tactfully worded. He obviously supports Auggie and admires Jack for defending him. Mr. Tushman addresses each of Mrs. Albans's "concerns" fairly and expresses his admiration for children with empathy, friendship, and loyalty—children like Jack Will.)*

6. How do the different media formats used in this section contribute to the novel's believability? *(Answers will vary. Between the letters, emails, Facebook messages, and text messages, the novel reflects modern society's reliance on various forms of digital communication while also suggesting that most formal communication still requires physical documentation [e.g., Jack's official letters explaining himself to Mr. Tushman and apologizing to Julian]. Portraying a Facebook friend request makes the novel seem more believable because the message is something most students are familiar with. The text messages between Auggie and Jack reflect shorthand that many students will likewise find familiar.)*

7. Why do you think Charlotte tells Jack about Julian's plot? *(Answers will vary. Charlotte has proven herself to be a kind person, so perhaps she feels it is cruel not to inform Jack of the situation. Some students might also speculate that Charlotte likes Jack romantically and thus informs him to gain his favor.)*

8. Why does Jack feel guilty for sitting with Summer and Auggie? *(Now that Jack is being ignored by most of the other fifth-grade students, he is uncomfortable sitting at his regular lunch table. When Summer and Auggie readily invite Jack to their table, he feels guilty that he wasn't always as nice to either of them. Specifically, he remembers dodging Auggie at lunch on the first day of school.)*

9. Why is Jack afraid to meet Auggie's family? *(Jack isn't sure what Auggie has told his family about Jack—and, specifically, if Auggie told them the mean things Jack said last Halloween. Jack also seems to think Via might remember him from the ice cream shop years before. Jack may also dread meeting Auggie's family because he is not sure what family dynamic exists in the Pullman household.)*

10. **Prediction:** How will Jack and Auggie's potato battery turn out?

Supplementary Activities

1. Art: Draw a "before and after" comparison of Jack's sled, *Lightning*.

2. Journal Entry: Think about a time when you had a chance to be especially kind to someone but you weren't. Write two to three paragraphs telling how the situation may have had different results if you had been kinder.

3. Music: Research zydeco music. What musical genres does zydeco blend to create its unique sound? Using online resources, find an appropriate audio or video clip demonstrating zydeco music. With your teacher's permission, play your clip for the class and list the most prominent sounds and instruments you hear.

Olivia's Brother–After the Show

Justin reveals his real first impression of Auggie and the Pullman family. He and Via prepare for a school production of *Our Town*. One day, as Justin walks Jack Will to the bus stop, he witnesses the harassment Jack suffers from classmates. Miranda reveals, to Justin's surprise, that she and Via were childhood friends, and Via confesses that she hopes Auggie will not attend the play. From Auggie's perspective, the reader learns of his and Jack's science fair success. Auggie's classmates grow tired of Julian's "war," and many begin speaking to Auggie and Jack again. After some initial doubts, Auggie grows accustomed to wearing hearing aids. The Pullmans tearfully say goodbye to their dog, Daisy, who has been gradually growing weaker. On *Our Town*'s opening night, Via stands in for Miranda as Emily Gibbs. Miranda reveals her life-changing experiences at summer camp, explaining why she and Via drifted apart. Happily, she describes how they reconnect after the school play.

Vocabulary
anomaly
immaculate
interjects
monologues
defensively
theorems
bionic
taciturn
ovation
collegiate
mayhem
euphoric

Discussion Questions

1. Why do you think the author omits capitals and some punctuation (e.g., quotation marks) in Part Five? *(Answers will vary. R.J. Palacio states on her Web site that she has always likened lowercase letters of the alphabet to notes on a musical staff. Therefore, Justin's all-lowercase chapter reflects his musicality. She attributes this unique analogy to her trombone-playing experience, as well as her career as a graphic designer. She also comments that she wrote Justin as a shy, quiet character who has more happening internally than externally. Thus, "the running monologue inside his head has no time for capital letters or punctuation: it's like his thoughts are streaming inside his mind.")*

2. Why is Justin surprised by Auggie's appearance, even though Via has described it? What does his actual reaction reveal about Justin? *(Though Justin knows about Auggie's condition, he expected that the numerous surgeries Via also mentioned would have made Auggie appear more normal. Answers will vary, but the fact that Justin is concerned about the effect his reaction will have on Auggie and Via shows that he is a kind, decent person. He shakes Auggie's and Jack's hands, compliments Auggie's room, and talks to the boys about his music, treating Auggie like any other kid.)*

3. What does Justin mean when he says that Via "is a girl who sees everything" (p. 191)? *(Justin means that Via is extremely observant as a result of growing up with Auggie. She is unusually*

sensitive to others' visual cues and reactions, so she notices things like Justin's tics and the waiter's expression when he sees Auggie. Students should note that Via, who is usually very vocal and protective of her loved ones, simply smiles and ignores any unpleasantness on this night.)

4. What does Justin realize about Jack as the two wait for the bus? How and why does Justin attempt to help Jack? *(After witnessing three boys harassing Jack, Justin realizes that Jack is shunned and regularly teased by his peers because of his friendship with Auggie. In an attempt to help Jack, Justin approaches the three boys and threatens that they "will be very, very, sorry" [p. 199] if they continue harassing Jack. Answers will vary. Though Justin claims that he doesn't know why he makes the threat, readers can conclude that Justin admires Jack's unwavering loyalty toward Auggie. Perhaps Justin, with his unique interests and difficult upbringing, also knows what it is like to feel singled out or isolated.)*

5. Do you empathize with Via as she confesses her feelings about Auggie to Justin? *(Answers will vary, but students should realize that Via, along with Auggie and her parents, has had to deal with people's reactions to Auggie's appearance her entire life. While her parents focused on Auggie, Via often had to fend for herself. As the child who was born with a "normal" face, she is considered lucky. And although she realizes that she was genetically lucky, she is not exempt from the stares, pointed fingers, and whispered comments that follow Auggie around. In fact, she is Auggie's fiercest defender. She does not complain often and now is simply expressing the relief she feels for not being identified by her relation to Auggie. Like Auggie, she simply wishes to feel "normal" sometimes.)*

6. What indicators signal that the "war" at Auggie's school is slowly ending? *(Auggie notices a decline in enthusiasm toward the war Julian started. Whereas Julian, Miles, and Henry initially played constant pranks on Jack [as pranks on Auggie would have been considered "bullying"] with nobody stopping them, people like Amos begin stepping in to stop the pranks. Many of the boys and nearly all of the girls in fifth grade are obviously tired of Julian's game. When Julian begins spreading a rumor that Jack hired a "hit man" [Justin] to threaten him and his friends, kids begin ridiculing Julian. Auggie observes that even Julian's two closest friends, Miles and Henry, are growing tired of the war.)*

7. What does Auggie mean when he says "…my ears were hearing brightly now" (p. 214)? Why is Auggie nervous to go back to school after seeing Dr. James? *(Auggie is trying to express the precision and clarity with which he is now able to hear. He marvels that he "could hear sounds like shiny lights in [his] brain" [p. 214] without also hearing an "ocean" of white noise. Auggie is nervous to return to school because he believes his new hearing aids, which are attached to a large headband, make him look like Lobot from* The Empire Strikes Back. *He thinks the hearing aids will give kids at school even more reason to stare at him.)*

8. How does Daisy's episode help Auggie gain some perspective? *(Answers will vary. When Auggie storms out of the kitchen after arguing with his mom and Via, he expects someone will come check on him in his bedroom. When Via enters to tell him about Daisy, Auggie does not consider that anything could be more important than his hurt feelings. Daisy's suffering immediately makes the dinner argument seem unimportant, and Auggie most likely realizes that although he may be upset, he is relatively healthy and should be thankful for that.)*

9. What do Miranda's "camp lies" reveal about her life and feelings? *(Answers will vary. Miranda's lies seem to mostly be taken from Via's life [e.g., that she lives in a townhouse in North River Heights, has a dog named Daisy, and has "a little brother who is deformed" {p. 237}]. It seems that Miranda envies Via's life, perhaps because Via has loving, concerned, attentive parents, while Miranda's parents are divorced and act distant toward her. It seems Miranda is an only child, so perhaps she wishes she had a sibling, too. At camp, Miranda lies to make herself more interesting to her peers. From the recent dramatic changes in her appearance [as well as the thoughts she reflects in Part Seven], the reader can conclude that Miranda suffers from low self-esteem.)*

10. Why do you think Miranda faked an illness just before the play? *(Miranda realizes that although she expects to do well in the play, none of her friends or family will be there to see it. After seeing Auggie enter the auditorium with his parents, she seems to realize that the part would mean much more to Via. Perhaps Miranda's actions partly stem from guilt, as well, since she pushed Via away after a summer apart. Students may also infer from Miranda's close bond with Auggie that her actions take his feelings into account, since seeing his sister onstage would surely make him happy.)*

11. **Prediction:** How will the "war" at Auggie's school end?

Supplementary Activities

1. Health: Justin suffers from tics, or muscle twitches, when he is nervous or stressed. Research different syndromes which list tics as a symptom (e.g., Tourette's syndrome, anxiety disorders, transient tic disorder), as well as different types of tics (e.g., motor tics, vocal tics). Prepare a brochure that might be distributed to young people with tics.

2. Critical Thinking: Compose a one- to two-page essay comparing the baroque violin (which Justin used to play) with the hardanger fiddle (which Justin now plays). Within your essay, explain why Justin's parents may not have noticed that he exchanged one for the other.

3. Art: Using magazine clippings, self-made art, and online images, create a collage illustrating Auggie's concept of "hearing brightly."

The Fifth-Grade Nature Retreat–Appendix

Auggie nervously prepares for his first overnight field trip. He enjoys the trip until several seventh graders begin harassing him and Jack in the woods during outdoor movie night. To Auggie's surprise, Amos, Henry, and Miles come to their aid. Auggie is glad to get home and thrilled when his dad and Via bring home a new puppy. When Auggie returns to school, he receives positive attention from his classmates, especially the athletes. Auggie has a candid conversation with Mr. Tushman about the school year and prepares for graduation. During the graduation awards ceremony, Auggie is presented with the Henry Ward Beecher medal and receives a standing ovation. Mr. Browne receives several precepts from Auggie's class after they graduate.

Vocabulary
detached
incantation
rappelled
concession
reimburse
seismic
attribution
ensemble
quantifiable
verbosity
exemplary
ruminating

Discussion Questions

1. Why is Auggie so anxious about the field trip to Broarwood Nature Reserve? *(Auggie has never spent a night away from home, except for during hospital stays. He is accustomed to having his parents near him at all times, since he often required specialized medical care that only doctors and his parents could provide. Once, when Auggie attempted a sleepover at his friend Christopher's house, he panicked and had to be picked up by his parents. In addition, Auggie is probably still apprehensive about Julian's war and how his classmates will treat him.)*

2. Why is the chapter about Auggie's encounter with the seventh graders titled "Alien"? *(Answers will vary, although the most obvious answer is that the seventh graders liken Auggie's appearance to the creatures from the movie* Alien. *However, the title may also refer to the situation itself. Auggie has always lived in a relatively*

safe neighborhood, and although he has been teased before, he has never found himself unsupervised and in physical danger. The chapter title may also relate to the "alien" feeling of being defended by Amos, Miles, and Henry—kids who, until this point, had been mean or neutral in their feelings toward Auggie and Jack.)

3. How is Mrs. Pullman's faith in people apparent in her conversation with Auggie in the kitchen? *(Mrs. Pullman claims she believes "that there are more good people on this earth than bad people, and the good people watch out for each other and take care of each other" [p. 279]. She seems to also believe that everyone has the ability to change for the better, saying "sometimes people surprise us" [p. 279].)*

4. How does Bear represent a new chapter in the Pullmans' lives? *(Answers will vary. Bear enters the Pullmans' lives at a very transitional moment. The family is still grieving Daisy's death, and adopting Bear helps them feel as if they are continuing Daisy's legacy. Auggie's parents are learning to let go of their son, allowing him to have his own experiences. Via is becoming a young woman, starting to date, making new friends, and finishing her first year of high school. Auggie is finishing fifth grade and is finally learning what it feels like to be accepted. In a sense, adopting Bear marks a turning point for each member of the family.)*

5. Describe the shift that Auggie experiences when he returns to school after the field trip. *(Because of the incident during the field trip, Auggie's classmates treat him differently. The athletes, especially Amos, all begin acknowledging Auggie and calling him "little dude." Julian falls out of favor since he skipped the field trip, and Miles and Henry desert Julian for Amos.)*

6. How do you think Mr. Tushman found out about Julian's bad behavior toward Auggie? *(Answers will vary, but students should note that Mr. Tushman is an extremely observant and involved principal. He speaks honestly to students on a regular basis and maintains constant communication with his students' parents. Also, teachers who witnessed incidents between students would have reported these to Mr. Tushman. Plus, Mr. Tushman most likely watches out for Auggie especially, due to Auggie's special circumstances and newness to the school.)*

7. Why did Auggie's dad throw away Auggie's astronaut helmet? Why is Auggie angry but ultimately understanding about his dad's actions? *(Auggie's dad threw away the helmet because it saddened him that his son felt he needed to cover up his face. He did not think hiding every day was good for his son. Auggie is initially angry that his father reveals this information so nonchalantly when, at the time the helmet was lost, Auggie was devastated and his mom was panicked. However, Auggie ultimately realizes that his dad's actions were based on love. Auggie forgives his dad, even jokingly threatening to blackmail him with the secret.)*

8. What does Mr. Tushman mean when he proclaims Auggie "the greatest…whose strength carries up the most hearts" (p. 304)? *(Answers will vary, but students should note the definition of "greatness" that Mr. Tushman reads, which expresses that greatness is not a measure of what a person can do with his/her strength, but rather of how he/she chooses to use it. Against the odds, Auggie has overcome many challenges during his fifth-grade year and, indeed, throughout his entire life. Though he often felt hurt, desperate, or shunned, Auggie persevered—his "quiet strength" propelling him. He was able to change people's perceptions with the "attraction of his own [heart]" [p. 304]. Mr. Tushman seems to feel that everyone at Beecher Prep became a better person for knowing Auggie.)*

9. What does Julian Albans's precept suggest? *(Answers will vary, but students should recall that Mr. Tushman claimed Julian was switching schools. Perhaps Julian realized that his terrible behavior would not help him make [or keep] friends and plans to change at his new school. Or, perhaps he plans to continue the same behavior in a new environment.)*

Supplementary Activities

1. Art: Using watercolors, chalk, or pencil, illustrate one of the following scenes from the novel.

   • "Giant trees that almost totally blocked out the sunlight. Tangles of leaves and fallen tree trunks...There was a slight fog, too, like a pale blue smoke all around us" (p. 257).

   • "I loved the way bits of fire dust would float up and disappear into the night air. And how the fire lit up people's faces...And how the woods were so dark that you couldn't see anything around you, and you'd look up and see a billion stars in the sky" (p. 258).

   • "The shadows were really long on the grass, and the clouds were pink and orange. It looked like someone had taken sidewalk chalk and smudged the colors across the sky with their fingers" (p. 259).

2. Word Study: Auggie refers to the "ginormous" trees at Broarwood Nature Reserve. In 2007, Merriam-Webster included the word "ginormous" in its collegiate dictionary. Research what requirements a word must meet to be eligible for inclusion in a Merriam-Webster dictionary. Then, make a list of three recent additions that you find surprising or amusing (e.g., "DVR," "smackdown," "man cave," "bucket list").

Post-reading Discussion Questions

1. What message does this novel send about being different? *(Acceptance is a major theme in the novel. Auggie is physically different than any child his age, and he learns to accept and celebrate those differences. Jack comes from a different economic background than most of his classmates, but he pushes that aside to focus on being a good friend to Auggie. Summer is different from her classmates in that she is not overly concerned with popularity and immediately accepts Auggie for who he is. The novel communicates that being different is not only okay, but something to be proud of.)*

2. Discuss how the following Mr. Browne precept encompasses one of the novel's main messages: "YOUR DEEDS ARE YOUR MONUMENTS" (p. 65). *(Answers will vary. The precept expresses that, above all else, people will be remembered by the things they do. In the novel, many people are cruel toward Auggie, some are indifferent, while others are kind [or learn to be kind]. Julian is vicious in teasing Auggie and Jack, and this negative attitude becomes his "monument." At the end of the novel, he is disliked by most of the students at Beecher Prep. In contrast, Auggie holds his head high, maintaining his courage and never lashing out at others for their spitefulness. At the end of the novel, Auggie is highly admired by the students and faculty at Beecher Prep, even receiving the Henry Ward Beecher medal for his show of strength. His perseverance becomes his "monument.")*

3. How does Auggie grow and change in the story? *(Answers will vary. At the beginning of the novel, Auggie is a frightened, sheltered boy who staunchly refuses to attend a normal school. He still sits in his mother's lap and is put to bed by one or both of his parents. However, by the end of the novel, Auggie has braved Beecher Prep for an entire year, gaining confidence and courage along the way. He squirms away from his parents' public affection and asks his father to drop the babyish nickname "Auggie Doggie." He goes to sleep on his own and is even comfortable spending the night away from home. His friends, teachers, and family have helped him reach a new emotional and mental maturity.)*

4. Do you think this novel's portrayal of adults is realistic? Why or why not? *(Answers will vary. Auggie's parents are loving and protective, seldom get angry, and hardly ever say the wrong things. In this way, they seem rather unrealistic. R.J. Palacio comments that the children's points of view throughout the novel construct characters such as Mr. and Mrs. Pullman and Mr. Tushman as "somewhat idealized," never giving voice to the adults' doubts, fears, or other negative thoughts. However, there are rare glimpses into the adults' true feelings, such as when Via witnesses her mother standing silently outside Auggie's room or when Auggie sees his father crying silently after Daisy's death.)*

5. What lessons does *Wonder* teach about loss? *(Answers will vary. Both literal and figurative losses occur throughout the novel. On the literal level, Auggie loses his dog Daisy after the vet discovers a growth in her stomach. He loses his close bond with his childhood friends when they begin attending different schools or move away. Figuratively, Auggie experiences a loss of innocence when he begins attending Beecher Prep. His parents' protective walls are demolished, and he experiences the full, brutal force of the world. Other characters experience loss, as well. Via loses her parents' attention when Auggie is born, as his condition necessitates their complete attention. Jack loses his friends after deciding to defend Auggie. Overall, the novel teaches that loss is not without gain, as each person who loses something in the novel gains something as a result—whether it is wisdom, knowledge, experience, etc.)*

6. How does Jack evolve from a character the reader questions into a character the reader roots for? *(Initially, Jack is recruited as part of the "welcoming committee" Mr. Tushman assembles to greet Auggie. From Jack's perspective, the reader learns that he was reluctant to agree to Mr. Tushman's request but does so because he fears what Auggie's fate will be at Beecher Prep without allies. Jack's character comes into question when Auggie overhears his terrible comments in*

Ms. Petosa's class on Halloween. When Jack realizes Auggie overheard him, he is immediately regretful. Jack again becomes a character the reader can root for when he stands up to Julian, sacrificing his own popularity to defend Auggie.)

7. Why do you think the author chose to write the novel using multiple perspectives? What are the pros and cons of a multiple-perspective format? *(Answers will vary but might include that the author wished to portray well-rounded characters, including their motivations, conflicts, personal histories, and internal struggles. It also seemed that the author was interested in exploring Auggie's effect on others and how their views changed over time. The author claims that although she initially meant to write only from Auggie's point of view, she realized that "to really explore Auggie's complete story, [she] would have to leave his head for a while." She also cites the influence of Faulkner's multiple-perspective* As I Lay Dying *as inspiration for using this format. Pros of using multiple perspective in a story include being able to give multiple "takes" on the same characters and situations [and avoiding what Palacio refers to as "the precocious kid who somehow knows things he isn't supposed to know"], creating suspense by revealing certain things to the reader that perhaps other characters don't know, and providing the reader with the widest overall understanding. Cons include the risk of one character "hijacking" the story, being able to create a linear time line, and writing the characters as individuals who, together, form a cohesive world.)*

8. Why doesn't Julian have his own chapter? *(Answers will vary, but students should note that Julian is the character who changes the least in the novel. As a close-minded character, Julian's point of view would not have contributed to Auggie's story in a positive way; therefore, he was not represented. The author refers to Julian as "an obstacle Auggie and his friends must get around." She claims, "I just couldn't give voice to Julian's ugly sentiments—in essence, to give a bully a platform...The book's not about [Julian] and how he became the mean-spirited kid he is. It's about Auggie, the boy he never bothers to get to know. As a result, Julian's voice has no place in the book.")*

9. How are Julian and Summer opposites? *(Julian is someone who only feels confident when he is criticizing someone else "below" him. He is highly concerned with his image and social status, and he feels he must always be with a group. In contrast, Summer's confidence is not determined by others' opinions of her. She doesn't put others down just to feel better about herself, and she is relatively unconcerned with popularity. She makes her decisions independently of her peers.)*

10. How is Auggie's changing hairstyle symbolic in the novel? *(At the beginning of the novel, Auggie sports a Padawan braid and long bangs that he uses to cover as much of his face as possible. Midway through the novel, Auggie cuts off his braid with no explanation. By the end of the novel, Auggie has cut his hair the shortest he has ever had it, and he even lets Via put some styling gel in it. Auggie goes from having a childish, longer haircut to a shorter, more mature-looking haircut. The fact that Auggie no longer feels the need to hide behind bangs is symbolic of how much his confidence has grown during the school year.)*

11. How does the title *Wonder* tie in with the novel? *(Answers will vary. As a noun, the word "wonder" can refer to a miracle or something awe-inspiring. As an adjective, the word "wonder" can mean exciting admiration or amazement by virtue of being outstandingly good. Both of these definitions can apply to Auggie. His birth and survival were miraculous. Indeed, the genetic factors that combined to cause his condition were extremely unlikely to happen. However, Auggie's physical appearance makes it necessary for Auggie to develop great strength of character, and for this reason, he is admired by most people he meets. It is a "wonder" that Auggie lived, that he had parents determined to make a good life for him, that he became well enough to attend a mainstream school, and that he won over the hearts of kids who once flinched at the thought of touching him. Most notably, at the end of the novel, Auggie's mom tells him, "You really are a wonder, Auggie. You are a wonder" [p. 310].)*

Post-reading Extension Activities

Writing

1. Write your own personal precept on an index card and, as a class, create a "Precept Wall" somewhere in the classroom.

2. Write the first few paragraphs of "Part Nine" in the novel from Jack's or Via's point of view.

3. Compose an alternate ending for *Wonder*. Share your alternate ending with the class, and discuss any plot holes or problems your new ending might create. If necessary, revise your alternate ending to be plausible.

4. Write an acrostic poem using one of the following characters' names: Auggie, Summer, Jack, Olivia.

Critical Thinking

5. Brainstorm an alternate title for the novel. Then, brainstorm a title for a sequel to the novel. Share your titles with the class, and vote on the best alternate and sequel titles.

Art

6. Draw an 8 × 12 pencil sketch of what you imagine North River Heights (Auggie's neighborhood) looks like.

7. Use a bulletin board to create a class collage with the theme "Overcoming Obstacles."

8. Draw a symbol that you feel embodies "quiet strength." Explain your symbol to the class in a short presentation.

9. Interview your school counselor about the best way to deal with bullies. Create a brochure with the information you learn.

Reading

10. Choose and read another novel about a child who is singled out for being different (e.g., *Freak the Mighty* by Rodman Philbrick, *I Funny* by James Patterson, *Rules* by Cynthia Lord, *Al Capone Does My Shirts* by Gennifer Choldenko). Compare and contrast your chosen literary work to *Wonder* in a one- to two-page essay.

Assessment for *Wonder*

Assessment is an ongoing process. The following ten items can be completed during the novel study. Once finished, the student and teacher will check the work. Points may be added to indicate the level of understanding.

Name _____ Date _____

Student   **Teacher**

_____   _____   1. Pretend you work for a newspaper, and write a review of *Wonder*.

_____   _____   2. Using the Venn Diagram on page 27 of this guide, compare and contrast Auggie and Jack.

_____   _____   3. Complete the Character Buzz Words activity on page 28 of this guide for Via. Then, use the words from your chart to write a descriptive paragraph about Via.

_____   _____   4. Complete the Conflict chart on page 29 of this guide.

_____   _____   5. Write an essay explaining the importance of the following precept to the novel: "Have no friends not equal to yourself" (p. 311). Use information from the novel to support your answer.

_____   _____   6. Use the Cause/Effect Chart on page 30 of this guide to show how Auggie's decision to attend Beecher Prep affected him.

_____   _____   7. Complete the Story Map on page 31 of this guide.

_____   _____   8. Identify four events that help develop Via's character in the novel. Explain in one to two paragraphs how these events help the reader understand Via better.

_____   _____   9. Choose a word, sentence, paragraph, or scene that you think best illustrates the author's main message in the novel. Write a paragraph explaining your choice.

_____   _____   10. Write a summary of the novel using at least ten vocabulary words.

I Predict...

Directions: Spend a few minutes looking at the cover of the novel and flipping through its pages. What can you predict about the characters, the setting, and the problem in the novel? Write your predictions in the spaces below.

The Characters	The Setting	The Problem

From the information you gathered above, do you think you will enjoy reading this novel? Circle your response on the scale below.

$$0 — 1 — 2 — 3 — 4 — 5 — 6 — 7 — 8 — 9 — 10$$

I will not like this novel.   I will really like this novel.

Explain your prediction on the lines below.

_____

_____

_____

_____

_____

_____

_____

Word Map

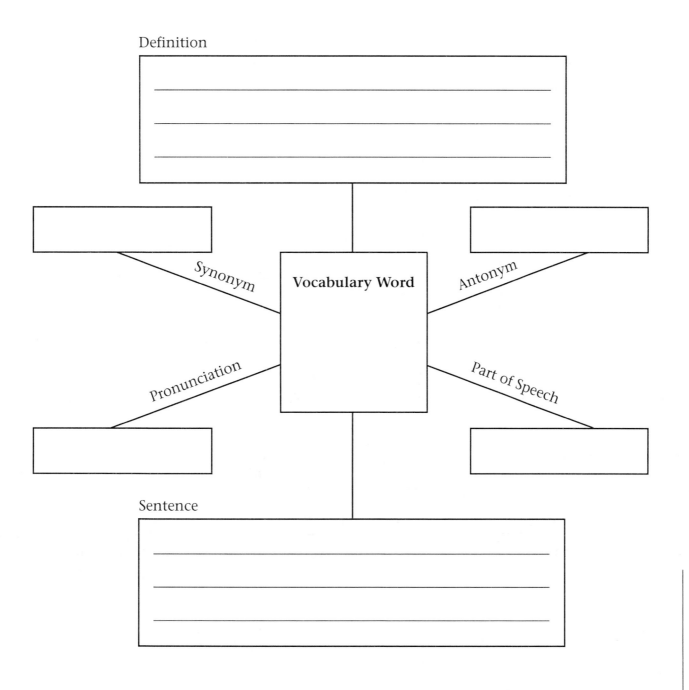

Definition

Synonym

Vocabulary Word

Antonym

Pronunciation

Part of Speech

Sentence

Character Web

Directions: Fill in information about Auggie in the chart below. Cite evidence from the story as you fill in information.

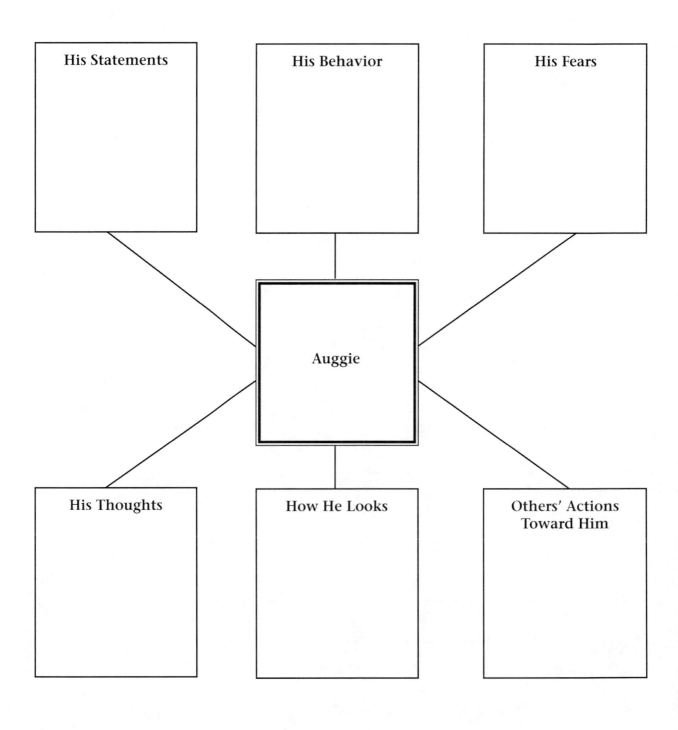

His Statements

His Behavior

His Fears

Auggie

His Thoughts

How He Looks

Others' Actions Toward Him

Venn Diagram

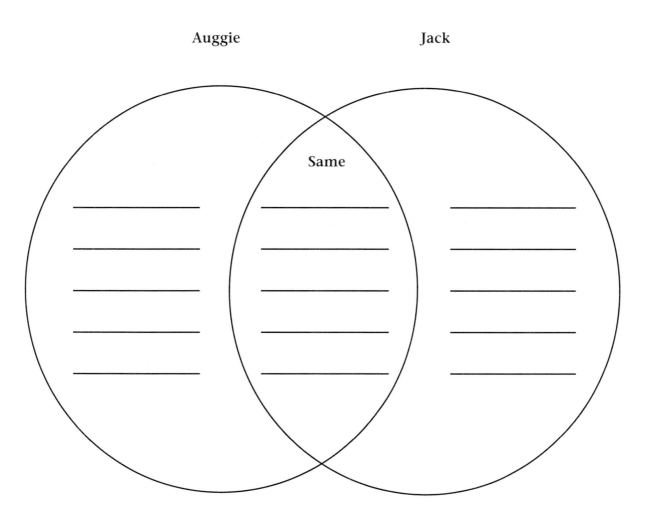

Auggie

Jack

Same

Character Buzz Words

Directions: In the graphic below, write as many words as you can think of to describe Via. Your words may describe Via's appearance, personality, emotions, demographics, etc.

Character: _____ Via _____

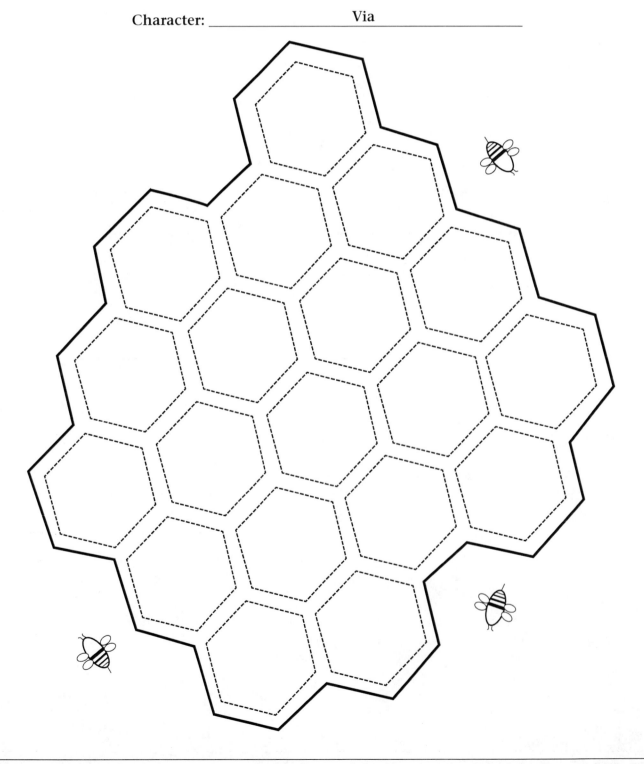

Conflict

The **conflict** of a story is the struggle between two people or two forces. There are three main types of conflict: person vs. person, person vs. nature or society, and person vs. self.

Directions: The characters experience some conflicts in the story. In the chart below, list the names of three major characters. In the space provided, list a conflict each character experiences. Then, explain how each conflict is resolved in the story.

Character:

Conflict	Resolution

Character:

Conflict	Resolution

Character:

Conflict	Resolution

Cause/Effect Chart

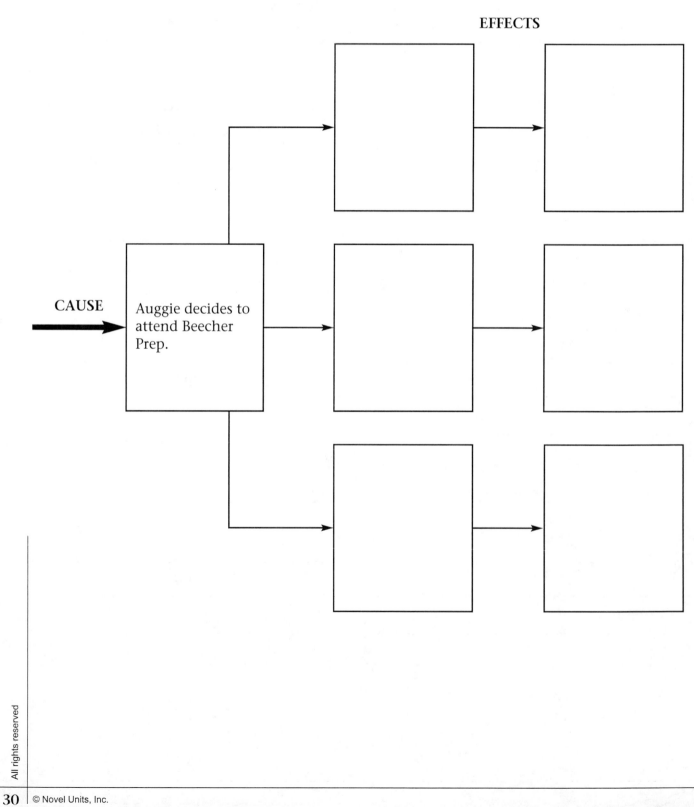

EFFECTS

CAUSE

Auggie decides to attend Beecher Prep.

Story Map

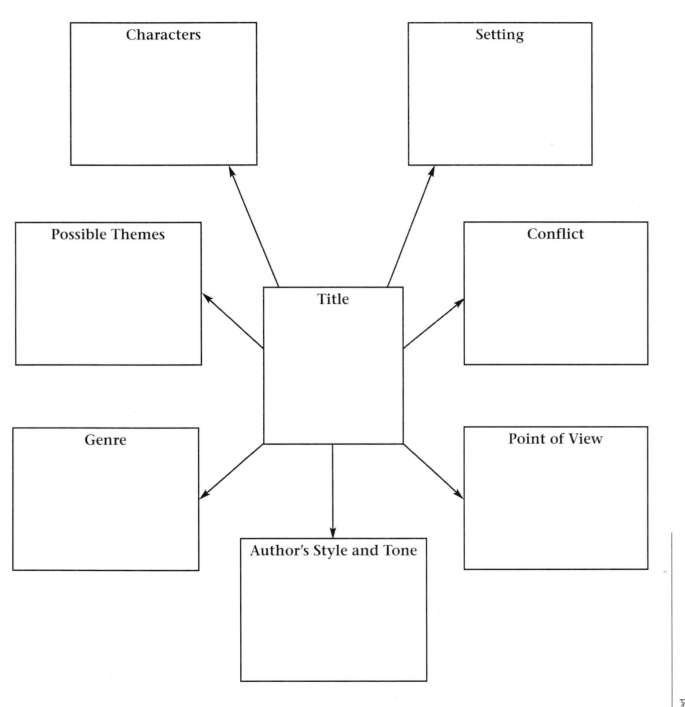

Characters

Setting

Possible Themes

Title

Conflict

Genre

Point of View

Author's Style and Tone

Linking Novel Units® Lessons to National and State Reading Assessments

During the past several years, an increasing number of students have faced some form of state-mandated competency testing in reading. Many states now administer state-developed assessments to measure the skills and knowledge emphasized in their particular reading curriculum. The discussion questions and post-reading questions in this Novel Units® Teacher Guide make excellent open-ended comprehension questions and may be used throughout the daily lessons as practice activities. The rubric below provides important information for evaluating responses to open-ended comprehension questions. Teachers may also use scoring rubrics provided for their own state's competency test.

Please note: The Novel Units® Student Packet contains optional open-ended questions in a format similar to many national and state reading assessments.

Scoring Rubric for Open-Ended Items

3-Exemplary
Thorough, complete ideas/information
Clear organization throughout
Logical reasoning/conclusions
Thorough understanding of reading task
Accurate, complete response

2-Sufficient
Many relevant ideas/pieces of information
Clear organization throughout most of response
Minor problems in logical reasoning/conclusions
General understanding of reading task
Generally accurate and complete response

1-Partially Sufficient
Minimally relevant ideas/information
Obvious gaps in organization
Obvious problems in logical reasoning/conclusions
Minimal understanding of reading task
Inaccuracies/incomplete response

0-Insufficient
Irrelevant ideas/information
No coherent organization
Major problems in logical reasoning/conclusions
Little or no understanding of reading task
Generally inaccurate/incomplete response